The Best Man

The Lessons That Fathers Have Not Taught Their Sons

Dr. Jesse W. Jackson III

Acknowledgements

My wife Kelly Lynn Jackson:
Thank you for challenging me to succeed and helping me to become the Best Man. I love and appreciate you.

My daughter, Kalynn:
Thank for bring so much joy to my life. This Best Man mission is to insure that your husband is properly trained and developed for the responsibility of taking care of a diva. You are beautiful and your father loves you very much.

Joshua And Kaleb "The Mountain Takers"
Thank you for the double blessing of twin boys. You are leaders and men of great influence. Thank you for the daily inspiration. I love you both.

My big brother, Lester Robinson:
Thank you for being a father to me. It is because you took me in as a son, that I am still alive. You guidance and protection save my life and motivated me to succeed. I am eternally grateful to you as a man and as a friend.

My first business coach, Johnny Stewart:
Thank you for teaching me the importance of entrepreneurship and business planning. The lessons you have taught me are the reason for my success.

Ralph Holley:
Thank you for taking interest in me as a youth and being a first class mentor. You have always been a great encourager in my life. I appreciate your years of love and support to our family. I love you and your family.

Jon Wynne:
Thank you for being a great teacher and friend. You are a great inspiration to me. Thank for the confidence you instilled in me. You are a big part of my success in life. Thank you.

Bill Winston:
Thanks for blessing my family and teaching me how to financially succeed.

The
Best
Man

The Lessons That Fathers Have Not Taught Their Sons
Dr. Jesse W. Jackson III

Plant A Seed Publishing & Media
Auburn Hills, Mi

Copyright © 2012 by Jesse W. Jackson III
All rights reserved.

Published Plant A Seed Publishing & Media
P.O. Box 210973
Auburn Hills, MI 48321

All rights reserved. Contents and /or cover may not be reproduced in whole or in part in any form without the express written consent of the Publisher.

Visit our Websites at www.jessejackson3rd.com and www.thebestmancompany.com.

Printed in the USA

ISBN 0-9762322-1-9

Library of Congress Control Number: 2009905681

3rd Edition: January 2012

Discounts on books are available for bulk purchases. To order this books for your business, church, college, or university, please write or call:

Best Man, LLC

P.O. Box 210973

Auburn Hills, MI 48321

1-888-261-3412
Please allow 1-2 weeks for shipping
Order online at: www.thebestmancompany.com

Table of Contents

Introduction   7

I. Purpose
Lesson 1 The Purpose Of Every Man   11
Lesson 2 Enemies Of Manhood   13

Ii. Education
Lesson 3 What Is A Good Man?   15
Lesson 4 What Is A Gentleman?   17

Iii. Health
Lesson 5 The Laws Of Good Male Hygiene   20
Lesson 6 The Purpose Of The Penis   22
Lesson 7 The Laws Of Sexual Responsibility   31

Iv. Business
Lesson 8 The Laws Of Leadership   36

V. Finance
Lesson 9 The Laws Of Male Financial Responsibility   40

Vi. Marriage
Lesson 10 The Male Guide For Responsible Dating   47
Lesson 11 What Every Man Must Know Before Getting Married   57
Lesson 12 The Roles And Responsibilities Of A Husband   65

Vii. Fatherhood
Lesson 13 The Roles And Responsibilities Of A Father.   71
Lesson 14 Every Man Must Stay Under The Authority Of A Senior (Mature, Wiser, And More Established) Male   76
Lesson 15 Grow Up!   77

M.A.N. School
Table of Contents

Introduction		**80**
I. Law 1	**Find Your Purpose And Live It**	85
Ii. Law 2	**Watch Your Mouth And Keep Your Word**	91
Iii. Law 3	**Maintain Sexual Self Control** "Keep It In Your Pants"	93
Iv. Law 4	**Be A Leader, Not A Follower**	95
V. Law 5	**Become Financially Free**	97
Vi. Law 6	**Find A Wife, Love Her And Give Her The Best Life**	100
Vii. Law 7	**Raise Your Children With Love And Affection, And Leave Them An Inheritance.**	101

The Best Man Daily Affirmation   103

Introduction

Every boy needs a man to teach him how to be a man. Fathers have God-given responsibilities to protect, educate, guide and set a good example for their children. Sadly, the trend of today's society is that millions of boys are growing up in homes without a father to teach and guide them. Many other boys are being raised by men who were not taught how to be men. Please consider these brutal facts and statistics from the National Fatherhood Initiative:

The Father Factor

- Children in father-absent homes are five times more likely to be poor. Source: U.S. Census Bureau,
- Even after controlling for income, youths in father-absent households still had significantly higher odds of incarceration than those in mother-father families. Youths who never had a father in the household experienced the highest odds.
Source: Journal of Research on Adolescence
- Youths are more at risk of first substance use without a highly involved father. Source: Social Science Research
- In a study of 6,500 children from the ADDHEALTH database, father closeness was negatively correlated with the number of a child's friends who smoke, drink, and smoke marijuana. Source: National Fatherhood Initiative.
- Fatherless children are twice as likely to drop out of school. Source: U.S. Department of Health and Human Services.

Source: www.fatherhood.org

These statistics should be very alarming to all of us. When a man does not know how to be a man, he makes it up as he goes along, or he finds other sources from which to learn. Those sources may or may not be appropriate. Boys who don't have a father to train and nurture them essentially gives them no chance at winning in the game of life. I believe being raised without the proper guidance and presence of a father is the biggest indicator of financial and social failure.

To address this massive problem that men all over the world are experiencing, we must attack and change the ideology of how we view and train men. Men are not brute beasts with a lack of self-control, who must have sex with every woman who will let them. All men have the potential to be wise sons, excellent husbands, responsible fathers, and strong leaders. After-school programs, prison, the military, and medication are not solutions for this epidemic of malehood illiteracy; but male education, accountability, guidance, and empowerment are the answer.

There are seven building blocks for every man alive. They are:

- Purpose: What you are born to do.
- Education: What you learn about what you were born to do.
- Business: How you expand what you were born to do.
- Finances: How you profit from what you were born to do.

- Health: How you take care of yourself while you are doing what you were born to do.
- Marriage: Finding a help mate (woman) to complete the mission.
- Fatherhood: Reduplicating yourself to expand and continue the mission.

I believe these seven areas will define a man's existence. Man is a creator with a great purpose, and when that purpose is unknown or neglected, abuse is inevitable. The purpose of this book is to provide boys and men of all ages, stages and situations in life with a blueprint for manhood success. This book will clearly identify:

- The purpose of every man.
- The enemies in manhood.
- What is a gentleman?
- What is a good man?
- The purpose of the penis.
- The laws of sexual responsibility.
- The laws of male leadership.
- The laws of male financial responsibility.
- The male guide for responsible dating.
- What every man must do before getting married.
- The roles and responsibilities of a husband.
- The roles and responsibilities of a father.

These valuable lessons will provide men and boys of all ages with proper guidance that will produce success in education, health, business, finances, marriage, and fatherhood. I learned all of these lessons after becoming a major failure in my life. I HAD PLENTY OF MEN OFFER ME THEIR PERSONAL experiences and theories on manhood, but very little of it produced success. There is more to manhood than having sex, watching sports, making money, and having children. Men have to be taught how to be "good" men, husbands, and fathers. God's intent was for our fathers to be our teachers. If you are a male that is without a father or have lacked the appropriate male role model in life, this book will be a tremendous help to you. These lessons will offer guidance to any man or boy who is willing to learn and will produce educational, health, business, financial, marital and fatherhood success.

Lesson 1
The Purpose of Every Man

Mankind was created by God, in the image of God, and his divine purpose for every man was for man to:

- Have control over his environment (not people); this is why we fight over territory, laws that govern the territory, and how we should live in the territory.
- Work by thinking, planning and speaking — this is why our words are so powerful.
- Be married, have a God-given wife, and use sexual intercourse for pleasure and to reproduce himself by having children. When a man takes a wife, he must depart his from his parents and reprioritize all of his relationships because his wife now comes first.
- Influence everyone around him.
- Operate his body on fruits, vegetables, and grains (every herb bearing seed).
- Be a steward of wealth.
- Protect his family in the environment.
- Guide his family.
- Develop his family.
- Have discipline and follow his God given purpose.

When men are taught these basic truths, they can govern their lives accordingly. When men do not know or live by these truths, it can be very destructive and nonproductive. Every man has a divine purpose for their life and without fulfilling it, they can never be truly happy. I suggest that every man take the time to find his purpose through quiet time, meditation, and soul searching. A good life is waiting on you, but it starts with your decision to live a purpose directed life.

Lesson 2
Enemies of Manhood Success

1. Pride.

Pride comes before every fall in a man's life. It is foolish to believe that you do not need anyone's help to succeed in life. Being prideful will cause a man to be shamed in his life. Pride is also the major cause of fighting and strife. Pride is fueled by a foolish tongue, but the lips of the wise preserve us. Pride is the root of all male downfalls, but honor is the result of humility. Humility is the way to success in life.

2. A lack of sexual control.

If a man cannot control himself and make wise decisions concerning his sexual conduct, his life will always be full of unnecessary problems. I will discuss this in more detail on Law Three, Maintain Sexual Self-Control.

3. Suppressed anger.

Unfortunately, men have been taught that it is unmanly to cry or express hurt feelings. This is why so many men are bitter and hostile. However, it has always been healthy to express how you feel without being angry. It is completely dangerous and unwise to hold your feelings inside.

4. Drinking alcohol and using drugs.

Alcohol and drugs are a major diversion from a deeper personal issue in a life. When men use drugs and alcohol, they are responsible for holding themselves back in life. Alcohol and drugs are for people who have problems and do not know how to deal with them. Alcohol and drugs have destroyed millions of men and their families. I suggest that you never drink alcohol or use any kind of drugs.

5. Poor communication.

Communication is a key element of life success. All men must learn how to effectively communicate their thoughts. A man who cannot effectively communicate in life will not be successful.

6. Negative peers.

Unfortunately, many men keep company with negative peers. This tends to happen because some men have low self-esteem and needs losers around for validation. Keeping bad company will bring trouble, cause poverty, and ruin your life.

I believe that most men need new friends. The saying "birds of a feather flock together" is completely true. I had to stop associating with many of my close friends and family members because we did not share the same values concerning life, marriage, manhood and money. I am not better than anyone else, but my desires were different and I was willing to do the work to get them. Your company should reflect your life goals. If you keep company with negative people who are not willing to go the extra mile for a better life, then you will be unsuccessful in life. Leaving old friends and family members is never easy, but it is necessary for any man who wants to be successful. Make a decision to separate from anyone or anything that will not fully allow you to sellout for total life success.

Lesson 3
The Principles of a Good Man

We often hear people say, "He is a good man." People base their theory of being a "good man" on their personal thoughts; however, it's wise to allow proven success principles to tell us what a "good" man really is. Here is a list of some qualities of a good man.

1. A good man knows his God-given purpose.
2. A good man is honest.
3. A good man is led by his God-given purpose.
4. A good man's mouth speaks only wisdom.
5. A good man is well insured and leaves an inheritance for his children and grandchildren.
6. A good man has favor with others.
7. A good man shows favor to others.
8. A good man will always win over his enemies.
9. A good man gives to the poor and his lifestyle brings him honor.
10. A good man honors and trusts God.
11. A good man's children are blessed after him.
12. A good man is empowered to prosper and gain wealth.
13. A good man is gracious and full of compassion.
14. A good man is smart and wise in his dealing.

15. A good man is firmly planted in his foundation, and his right way of living will be remembered forever.

16. A good man is mature in his love walk and has no fear.

17. A good man is hated by many, but respected by all.

Lesson 4
Be A Gentleman

Every man has a responsibility to be and conduct himself like a gentleman at all times. Here are some basic guidelines that a gentleman should follow in his personal life and in the presence of a lady.

1. **Always open doors.**
   This is the most basic rule of male etiquette. A gentleman should always open the door for a woman when they enter your car, restaurant, or anyplace with a door. No excuses!
2. **Help her with her coat.**
   Always help a lady put her coat on or over garment.
3. **Always assist with her seat.**
   It is important that you help her be seated by pulling her chair out and gently pushing it back into place when she is comfortable.
4. **Give up your seat.**
   If there is a lady present, and there are no available seats, you should stand up and offer yours immediately.
5. **Stand at attention.**
   Always stand when a lady enters or exits the room. This is a powerful sign of respect. There has been some confusion concerning this principle, but I suggest that you stand upon entrance but remain seated upon exit, or you can do both.
6. **Give her your arm.**
   When escorting a lady, you should offer her your arm.

7. **Ask if she needs anything.**
   Always make sure to ask the lady if you can get her something to drink (or eat, depending on the event). I suggest doing everything to let the woman know that you care about her comfort and needs.
8. **Never groom yourself in public.**
   This includes picking your nose, chewing your nails and picking your teeth. These areas should only be ventured in private. Committing these acts overtly is a colossal mark of a lack of class.
9. **Be punctual.**
   Perhaps the greatest sign of respect, which is what a gentleman is all about, is being on time. Having people wait for you is the equivalent of telling them that you don't care about them.
10. **Shake hands firmly.**
    Your handshake should mirror your personality. You want the other person to think of you as someone resolved, concrete and positive. But it shouldn't be a test of your strength; don't hurt them. Your grip should be the same for women.
11. **Apply constant verbal grace.**
    Use "excuse me" or "I beg your pardon" for all occasions. An extension of politeness, you should always use these expressions, whether it's to get someone to move out of your way, to apologize for your upcoming journey to the men's room, or simply to signal your interlocutors that you're about to start a sentence.
12. **Tip well and discreetly.**
    When you do tip, don't be cheap. Respect the

15% gratuity for restaurant tabs and nothing less than $10 for a significantly useful maitre d'.

Gentlemen, these are the guidelines of being a gentleman that you should practice in everyday life. Your wife, daughter, and/or your female interest will appreciate it.

Source: By Michael Bucci "Etiquette Of A Gentleman: Part I" http://www.askmen.com/money/successful/41b_success.html.

Source: By John Samuel, "Etiquette Of A Gentleman: Part II", http://www.askmen.com/money/successful_60/66_success.html

Write down what you believe are your best gentleman qualities.

_____
_____
_____
_____
_____
_____
_____
_____
_____

Lesson 5
The Laws of Good Male Hygiene

Every man must understand the importance of taking care of his hygiene. These are some essential laws of good male hygiene.

1. Take a bath/shower at least once a day.
2. Wash your feet.
3. Wash in between your toes.
4. Cut your finger and toenail at least once every two weeks.
5. Change underwear and socks everyday.
6. Do not put on deodorant or cologne without taking a bath or showering.
7. Clean out your ears with a q-tip every day.
8. Wash your face in the morning.
9. If you have a beard, shave everyday.
10. Brush your teeth after every meal if possible; if not, make sure you brush your teeth at least twice a day.
11. Use toothpaste to brush your teeth.
12. Floss your teeth daily.
13. Properly wipe your buttocks to prevent bowel movement stains in your underwear.
14. Wash your hands before and after you urinate.
15. Iron your clothes.
16. Always keep breath mints and use them for fresh breath.

17. Wash your clothes with laundry detergent only.
18. Brush or comb your hair as needed.
19. Get hair cuts at least every 10 days.
20. Cut your nose hairs.
21. Always smell fresh.

Write a list of hygiene habits you need to improve and how you plan to do it.

_____
_____
_____
_____
_____
_____
_____
_____
_____
_____
_____
_____

Lesson 6
The Purpose of The Penis

This lesson clearly defines God's purpose for the male penis. So many boys and men alike were taught to refer to their penis as a **"Dick," "Cock," "Wiener," "Pee Pee," "Sausage," "Meat," "Knob," "Peter," "Pole," "Woody," or "Bone."** These slang terms are all inappropriate and have created lewd view of sex and the male body.

This book will clearly define why men were made with a penis and what He expects men to do with it. This is an excellent resource to assist parents in teaching young males the proper use of their penis.

God Has 3 Specific Purposes For The Penis

1. The purpose of the penis is to discharge urine.

Merriam Webster dictionary helps us to understand one of the purposes of the penis with its definition, "a male organ of copulation that in male mammals including humans usually functions as the channel by which urine leaves the body." Urine is defined as, "A waste material that is secreted by the kidney in vertebrates, is rich in end products of protein metabolism together with salts and pigments, and forms a clear amber and usually slightly acid fluid in mammals."

Definitions Source: Merriam Webster Dictionary

2. The purpose of a penis is for a <u>married man</u> to insert into his wife's <u>vagina</u> for sexual pleasure under the holy covenant of marriage.

To be married means, "the state of being united to a person of the opposite sex as husband or wife in a consensual and contractual relationship recognized by law."

Definitions Source: Merriam Webster Dictionary

3. The purpose of the penis is to transport <u>a married man's reproductive semen</u> into his <u>wife's vagina</u> for the purpose of conception of a human life.

Semen is defined as, "a viscid whitish fluid of the male reproductive tract consisting of spermatozoa suspended in secretions of accessory glands."

Definitions Source: Merriam Webster Dictionary

The Improper Use For The Penis

1. The penis is not to be placed in <u>any anus or rectum area</u>.

Rectum is defined as, "the terminal part of the intestine from the sigmoid flexure to the anus." The rectum is the part of the body in which toxic waste exits. Placing your penis in a rectum is the same as putting your penis in a garbage dump.

Definitions Source: Merriam Webster Dictionary

Syphilis continues to increase in men

The national rate of primary and secondary (P&S) syphilis – the early stages of the disease that indicate recent infection – has increased every year since an all-time low in 2000. **While surveillance data is not available by risk behavior, a separate CDC analysis suggests that approximately 64**

percent of all adult P&S <u>syphilis cases in 2004 were among men who have sex with men, up from an estimated 5 percent in 1999.</u>

Source: Center for Disease Control: www.cdc.gov

2. The penis is not for having sex with another male.

3. The penis is not intended to be placed <u>in more than one vagina in a man's lifetime</u>. There is a God designed female spouse for every man that has ever been born. Your penis was made to fit perfectly into that woman's vagina only.

4. The penis was not intended to be used with a condom.

The **purpose** of a **condom** is to catch **married men's** ejaculation during sexual intercourse with his wife, NOT TO GUARD YOU AGAINST DISEASE. Today's modern society promotes condoms as a way to have sex and prevent the spread of disease and unwanted pregnancy. However, this a horribly weak message to send to future of our nation. Promoting "safe sex", is like encouraging armed robbers not to shoot the person they rob. Unless you are married, a person's body does not belong to you. Sex is for married people and there is no sex safe outside of an God honoring marriage covenant.

5. The penis is not for fathering children out of wedlock.

6. The penis is not for having sex with animals.

7. The penis is not for having sex with relatives or family members.

8. The penis was not intended to be shared with every woman that will allow a male to enter her vagina, mouth, or rectum.

9. The penis is not for having sex with your wife during her menstrual cycle.

10. The penis is not for having sex by force or rape.

11. The penis is not to be used for masturbation, any form of pornography, or lewd sexual acts.

12. The penis is not intended for having sex with another man's wife.

13. The penis is not for having sex with children.

The Consequences Of The Misuse Of The Penis

1. Sexually Transmitted Diseases: AIDS, HIV, Syphilis, Gonorrhea, and Chlamydia are all results of the misuse of the penis.

- **Chlamydia is a common sexually transmitted disease (STD) caused by the bacterium,** *Chlamydia trachomatis*, **which can damage a woman's reproductive organs. Chlamydia can be transmitted during vaginal, anal, or oral sex.**

- **Gonorrhea is a sexually transmitted disease** caused by *Neisseria gonorrhoeae*, a bacterium that can grow and multiply easily in the warm, moist areas of the reproductive tract, including the cervix (opening to the womb), uterus (womb), and fallopian tubes (egg canals) in women, and in the urethra (urine canal) in women and men. **The bacterium can also grow in the mouth, throat, eyes, and anus.**

- Syphilis is a sexually transmitted disease (STD) caused by the bacterium *Treponema pallidum*. **Syphilis is passed from person to person through direct contact with a syphilis sore. Sores occur mainly on the genitals, vagina, anus, or in the rectum. Sores also can occur on the lips and in the mouth. Transmission of the organism occurs during vaginal, anal, or oral sex.**

- Reported cases of sexually transmitted disease by sex: United States, 2004

	Male	Female	Total
Chlamydia	210,396	716,675	929,462
Gonorrhea	157,303	172,142	330,132
Primary Syphilis	2,026	241	2,269
Secondary Syphilis	4,696	1,014	5,711
Early Latent Syphilis	5,433	2,331	7,768
Late and Late Latent Syphilis ‡	10,340	6,896	17,300
Neurosyphilis	650	182	833
Chancroid	19	9	30

2. Illegitimate children and single parent homes are the result of the misuse of the penis. However, it is important to identify that a large number of women are <u>deliberately</u> getting pregnant to become a mother without a husband.

- Nearly 20 million children (27 percent) live in single-parent homes.
- 1.35 million births (33 percent of all births) in 2000 occurred out of wedlock.
- Over 3.3 million children live with an unmarried parent and the parent's cohabiting partner. <u>The number of cohabiting couples with children has nearly doubled since 1990, from 891,000 to 1.7 million today.</u>

Source: National Fatherhood Initiative

3. The misuse of the penis has caused deficiencies in children's education.

Even after accounting for differences in income, **children who were born out of wedlock and either remained in a single-parent family or whose mother subsequently married had significantly poorer math and reading scores and lower levels of academic performance than children from continuously married households.**

Source: Cooksey, Elizabeth C. "Consequences of Young Mothers' Marital Histories for Children's Cognitive Development." Journal of Marriage and the Family 59(May 1997): 245-261.

4. The misuse of the penis has caused poverty.

<u>**Single-parent families are five times as likely to be poor as married-couple families**</u>. In 1999, 6.3 percent of married-couple families with children were living in poverty, compared to 31.8 percent of single-parent families with children.

Source: U.S. Census Bureau. Current Population Survey.

5. For most men, <u>Child Support</u> is the result of the misuse of a penis.

6. Domestic violence is the result of the misuse of the penis.
There are very few if any cases of domestic violence with unmarried couples that are not having sex.

- **Marriage dramatically reduces the risk that mothers will suffer from domestic abuse.** The incidence of abuse by a spouse, boyfriend, or domestic partner is twice as high among mothers who have never been married as it is among mothers who have been married (including those who have separated or divorced).
- **Marriage dramatically reduces the prospect that mothers will suffer from violent crime in general at the hands of intimate acquaintances or of strangers.** Mothers who have never married--including those who are single and living either alone or with a boyfriend, and those who are cohabiting with their child's father--are twice as likely to be victims of violent crime as are mothers who have been married.

Source: Robert E. Rector, Patrick F. Fagan, and Kirk A. Johnson, Ph.D., "Marriage: Still the Safest Place for Women and Children," Heritage Foundation Backgrounder No. 1732, March 9, 2004.

7. Adultery is always the result of the misuse of the penis and your brain.

Male's Must Honor Their Penis!

It is important to never forget that your penis is a vessel of life and should be handled as carefully as a loaded gun. The purpose of your penis is to urinate, pleasure your wife and create a family with her only. Any function outside of these will always make you subject to disastrous consequences.

Parents must teach their sons early in life that their penis is sacred and should only be shared with their wife.

The Lower Male Anatomy

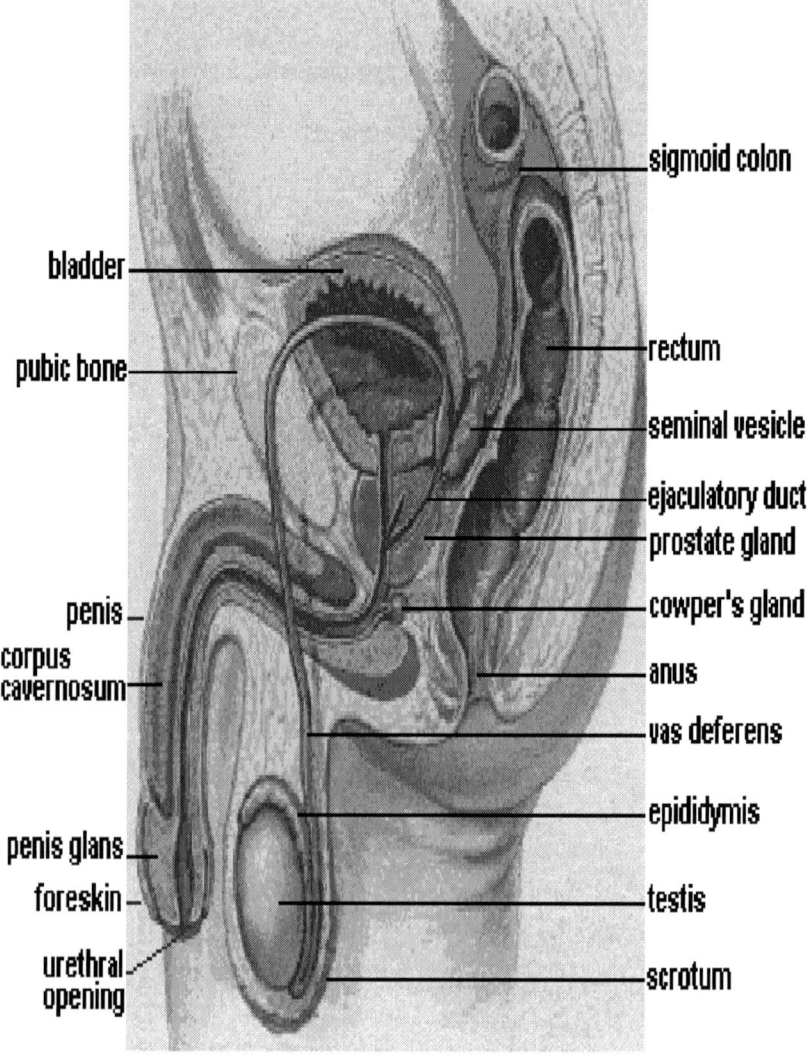

The Best Man/ 7 Laws of Male Success

Lesson 7
The Laws of Male Sexual Responsibility

1. Never entertain the conversation of a loose woman.
A loose woman is one who is willing to having sex with any man. Loose women like to hug and flirt with men. A loose woman's goal is to get a man's attention by any means necessary. It is wise to avoid any woman you know is loose in speech, conduct, dress, or sexual morality.

2. Do not depend on willpower or self-control to keep you out of sexually compromising situations.
No man can consistently overcome his attraction or the advances of a woman he finds attractive. It is wise to use good judgment before any opportunities to have sex with a woman you are not married to. Stay out of these positions!

3. What we think about, we will talk about.
Our words set things in motion. Talking sexually explicitly about sex outside of your marriage is a sexual misconduct seed. We must account for every word that comes out of our mouths. I suggest that you save all of the sex talk for your wife.

4. Dating is an interview for marriage, not a chance to have a sex partner.
The purpose of dating is to prepare and explore the possibilities of marriage to a specific person.

Any man who is dating a woman to have sex with her does not care about her or himself. **Every human being knows in his spirit (conscience) that pre-martial sex is wrong.** Pre-marital sex has disastrous consequences on your spirit, mind, emotions, and physical body. Sex is a spiritual activity, which joins together spirits and makes a man and woman one flesh. <u>Sex makes marriages legal. This process is and should be reserved for those who have totally committed themselves to each other under the covenant of marriage.</u> **If you are ready to have sex then you should get married and do it the RIGHT WAY!** It is selfish to take a woman's body without committing to her all that you have in marriage.

A man must keep himself out of positions in which he is vulnerable to his attraction or the advances of a woman. There is not enough willpower in the world to save a man from his desire for a woman. Therefore, it is important to stay out of those positions, which will put pressure on you to have sex with a woman you are not married to. A real man cares about a woman he is dating and respects her body. It is wise for a man to save himself for his wife.

5. Refrain from coarse joking, obscene gestures, or any sexual references to anyone, particularly women.

6. Always be aware that loose women dress and wear clothes to get your attention.

7. It is wise to be conscious of how you dress in the workplace or at school.

Some women like to inappropriately look at men's private parts through their pants; therefore, men should be conscious of this and dress appropriately. It is also inappropriate for a man to have his shirt open where women can see his chest hair. This can be perceived as sexually suggestive. I suggest that you take every precaution necessary to protect yourself in this area.

8. Be wise when complimenting women.

Not all women can receive friendly compliments. It is unwise to leave yourself open to potential sexual harassment complaints due to your kindness. It is not worth it.

9. Do not practice hugging or kissing other women.

Once again, this is a protective measure. A man should refrain from being loose and giving hugs to other women. We have often seen this behavior as harmless, but exchanging hugs sends messages of love, intimacy, and respect. Hugs can violate personal boundaries and mislead people. Loose women take great pleasure in hugging a man. I believe that men must be extremely careful in this area and make wise decisions that will protect them against any allegation.

10. Do not drink alcohol with women.

Alcohol impairs people's judgment and makes men and women vulnerable to immoral sexual conduct. I suggest that you stay out of this position at all times.

11. Consider never going to strip clubs.

These activities are a foolish waste of money. They bring temporary gratification, but always produce financial shortage and other legal problems.

One example: "Stephen Jackson, the Indiana Pacers' guard, was charged with a felony for criminal recklessness and misdemeanor counts of battery and disorderly conduct Wednesday by the Marion County prosecutor, five days after he fought with another group of men outside a strip club."
Source: ESPN.com news services Associated Press, Oct. 12, 2006

12. Always keep an appropriate distance in verbal communication and maintain appropriate personal space boundaries.

A man should not stand over or walk behind a woman in a way that it can be perceived he is watching her.

13. Have control over your eyes.
Watching pornography, viewing Internet porn, reading pornographic magazines, watching the

Playboy channel and performing lewd masturbation are all very dangerous sexual misconduct seeds. The world teaches us that it is OK to "look, but don't touch." However, this is a trap for men to fall into sexual immorality. I want to encourage you to guard your eyes and ears against sexually provocative material.

Lesson 8
Laws of Leadership
Mandatory, Non-Negotiable Qualities And Characteristics Of A Successful Leader

Men of all ages must understand that society needs men to be leaders not followers. I believe that men have a responsibility to be leaders, whether it is in his business, politics, education or the military. However, every man has a primary leadership responsibility in their own home first. After years of leadership research and practice, I have found that every male leader must possess these four non-negotiable character traits to be considered for any level of leadership.

1. A true leader must be faithful to his wife. If a man will cheat on his wife, with whom he is in covenant with, then he is a threat to cut anyone's throat. A man who is unfaithful to his wife is not trustworthy and should never be trusted to lead anything of value.

2. A true leader cannot be a thief. How can we trust a thief? If a man is proven to be a thief, then he should be disqualified from all leadership positions.

3. A true leader cannot abuse alcohol or other mind alternating substances. If a man chooses to drink alcohol and use drugs, he puts himself in a vulnerable position to poor discretion in situations with loose women. A drunk always has an excuse for his behavior, and real leaders do not make excuses. A leader who likes to drink alcohol is a risk to sell out those he is leading when he gets drunk.

4. A true leader must rule his house well. If a leader does not have the respect of his wife and children, he is not qualified to lead. If a man's children do not respect him, he has clearly failed at home and needs to spend more time there before can guide someone else.

These leadership principles should be observed by all leaders, including government officials (presidents, Senators, governors, mayors and Congressmen), husbands, pastors, principals, policemen, sheriffs, coaches, CEOs, and all management. I believe if we hold leaders to these standards, our businesses, schools, churches, and governments would dramatically change for the better immediately. Here are 25 basic leadership principles that I believe all men must understand and live by.

Leadership Principles

1. **All leaders need God's help.**
2. Sound **leadership** has a moral foundation.
3. **Leaders** can cause people to err and to be destroyed.
4. The mark of a good **leader** is loyal followers; **leadership** is nothing without a following.

5. A good **leader** motivates, doesn't mislead, doesn't exploit.

6. A good **leader** abhors wrongdoing of all kinds.

7. Good **leaders** cultivate honest speech; they love advisors who tell them the truth.

8. An intemperate **leader** wreaks havoc in lives; you're smart to stay clear of someone like that.

9. Good-tempered **leaders** invigorate lives.

10. A good **leader** does not lie, cheat, or steal.

11. Love and truth form a good **leader.**

12. Sound **leadership** is founded on loving integrity.

13. A good **leader** should hate corruption.

14. A **leader** of good judgment gives stability

15. An exploiting **leader** leaves a trail of waste.

16. When a **leader** listens to malicious gossip, all the workers get infected with evil.

17. **Leadership** gains authority and respect when the voiceless poor are treated fairly.

18. Promiscuous women will destroy a **leader.**

19. **A leader** can't afford to make fools of themselves by getting drunk.

20. A city without wise **leaders** will end up in ruin.

21. A city with many wise **leaders** will be kept safe.

22. In time of war there are many **leaders**, but a sensible **leader** restores law and order.

23. A heartless **leader** is a fool.
24. A nation will prosper when its **leader** is mature.
25. Bad **leaders** destroy families.

Lesson 9
The Laws of Male Financial Responsibility

Financial responsibility is vital to every man's success in life. Without the understanding of financial education and intelligence, a man will always be broke and keep his family broke. Here are 17 of the most important laws of a male's financial responsibility.

1. Know your purpose.

I have learned that financial freedom is connected to knowing and living out your purpose. Many men waste time and energy working in irrelevant jobs when they should be walking in their purpose, which will produce far more financial results.

2. Start your life with a financial exit strategy (How you want to end up financially).

Financial goals are necessary for every man. It is important to take the time research how much money you need for all of the things you desire to do in your life before you start.

3. Mind your own business.

Once again, I do not feel it is wise to invest all of your life working for someone else. Every man must understand that he has a responsibility to mind his own business first. Minding your business simply means that you are contributing your time and money into building your financial future, not making others rich.

4. Pay yourself first – investing.

10 percent of every dime you make should be invested into your personal business endeavors.

5. Pay bills on time.

It is an act of great integrity to always pay your bills on time.

6. Take care of your credit.

Good credit is a very important factor in financial success. Good credit means your word is good. It also means that you will do what you say you will do. Good credit allows you to buy whatever you need with other peoples' money. Be responsible and take the time to learn the proper use of your credit and borrowing money. http://www.citibank.com/us/cards/cm/

7. Fully insure your family with all forms of insurance (life, short-term disability, property, stocks).

Every man must have short-term disability coverage and a life insurance policy of at least $500,000 for his wife and $500,000 for each child. Until you build your assets to pay all of your income every month, this will protect your family against hardship in the case of your premature death.

8. College planning.

Every father has the responsibility to pay for his children to go to college. For most men, this will require a lot of planning and extra work. This is why you must start early and never neglect this duty.

9. Do not be lazy!
If you are in a bad financial situation, you can't be lazy. Certain situations may call for a man to work two jobs until he is financially educated enough to create passive or portfolio income to pay his monthly expenses. A man cannot sit around or depend on his wife's income to support the family because he is too lazy to learn and do more to improve his family's financial situation. It is very dishonorable to send your wife to work to "help you" pay your bills. There are no excuses for this. Until you get in a better position, then you do what is necessary to provide for your family.

10. Stop wasting money on lottery tickets, casinos, Keno, and sports betting. Once again, I am talking to people with no money to spare, not Tiger Woods or Charles Barkley! They gamble as a recreation. Most gamblers are lazy people looking for a quick fix to financial freedom. This is typically the type of person who will win two million dollars and end up broke within a year. This is a foolish waste of money.

11. Increase the time you spend on financial education.

I recommend that you read and listen to all of Robert Kiyosaki's "Rich Dad Poor Dad" books and audio books. You can start by going to your local library and checking them out. Without financial education, you have no chance of improving your financial situation.

12. Invest in your marriage!

Go to marriage seminars, retreats, and value your spouse. Typically, a married man who does not treat his wife well will always be broke. This is a very serious issue that affects your financial situation. Investing in your marriage will always pay a high return. The better your marriage is, the more money you will be able to make.

13. Do not ever quit your job without a better one to replace it.

Millions of men have foolishly quit their jobs based on how they felt. This can create financial hardship and force your wife to leave you because of your stupidity. This is not wise!

14. Do not keep company with poor people.

Our company is a reflection of our mentality and we cannot afford to surround ourselves with people who have a poverty mentality or lifestyle.

15. Live on 70% of your income. For example, if you make $40,000 a year, you should be living on $28,000 a year. The 40% pays 10% in tithes, 10% to yourself, 5% for short-term savings and 5% for emergencies. This will also ensure that you will always have money in emergencies. We suggest that you pay yourself first. Meaning take out a percentage of your income and pay it to yourself for an investment. Do not spend that money until it is time to a purchase income generating investment.

16. This is how your monthly budget should look until you have a change of financial status:

Monthly Budget	Expense
Tithes 10%	
Personal saving 20% (5% short term, 5% emergency, and 10% business investments)	
Debt repayment 5%	
Housing (rent, utilities, insurance) 25%	
Food 15%	
Auto 10%	

Insurance 3%	
Entertainment 2%	
Clothing 3%	
Medical 2%	
Marriage enrichment 5%	

- If you find that your house or living arrangement exceeds 40% of your income, you are in a financially destructive situation (you are living above your means).
- If you find that your automobile expenses exceed 10% of your monthly income, sell your car or change vehicles.
- Stop all spending and make a written budget to track every cent you spend.

17. Live a life directed toward your God-given purpose.

The root cause of being broke is failing to live in accordance with your God-given purpose. Poverty is inevitable without purpose, and purpose without the work to back it up will always lead you to poverty. I am advising you to take these three fundamental steps:
1. Find out the will of God for your life.
2. Once you find it, do not confer with others' opinions or theories about it.
3. Get the job done at all cost.

This is how I became financially free. Fulfilling your life's purpose will bring the blessing of the Lord that make us very rich and adds no sorrow to it!

Write your 12-month financial goals and the plan to accomplish them.

_____
_____
_____
_____
_____
_____
_____
_____
_____
_____
_____
_____
_____
_____
_____
_____
_____
_____
_____
_____
_____
_____
_____
_____
_____

Lesson 10
The Male Guide To Responsible Dating

Dating is an interview for marriage. The purpose of dating is to prepare and explore the possibilities of marriage to a specific person. Merriam Webster Dictionary defines dating or courting as "<u>engaging in social activities leading to engagement and marriage</u>." Contrary to popular belief, dating is still a sacred process. The purpose of dating is not just to have fun or to look for a new person to have sex with. The goal of dating should always be marriage, or you are just wasting time.

All marriages must be birthed and conceived by the man. If a man does not want to get married or is not ready for marriage, we can guarantee you that the marriage will be an absolute failure. Men are the foundation of marriage, and women are to complete the foundation. Today's married couples are experiencing a great deal of unhappiness because so many married men were not ready for marriage. We believe there are five basic dating benchmarks (starting points) for a man. A man should only be dating or courting a woman, if he:

1. Knows his purpose for his life.

2. Has begun carrying out a purpose-driven vision (plan) for his life.

3. Has a stable job (means to support a family).

4. Has his own transportation (not public transportation).

5. Has his own suitable living arrangement (not with the opposite sex or with his mother).

This is the starting point. These are foundational benchmarks that will govern what kind of husband he becomes. **It is important to always understand that the way you date will set the tone for your marriage.** I want you to *Do It Right The 1st Time*. Here are 13 of the most important things that a man should understand about dating responsibly.

1. If you are not working (legally employed), you should not be dating.

Money is required to date. Stable and legal employment allows a man to consistently provide for a family. This is one of the most important things that a man has to do for himself.

A woman is a gift from God and her presence should be a reward for a man. A man should be in position to be a blessing to the woman for her allowing him to share her presence. The responsibility of work comes along with having a woman (wife). This should be your primary focus before ever attempting to date. **A lazy man does not deserve a date and no woman should be paying his way.**

2. Pay the bill.

Contrary to popular belief, a man should always pay for all activities when dating. A man is the person who should be doing the courting, so he should pay for all of the dating activities. Therefore, go to places that you can afford.

In dating, a man's role is to show the woman what the benefits will be of marrying him. A woman should always know that she will be well taken care of by her husband. A man should not take advantage of a woman's low self-esteem, which encourages her to validate her independence and value by spending money on a man. **This is why so many women take guys out, drive them around in their cars, and let them move in with them.**

Dating is the process that builds marital expectations. This type of behavior is dangerous and will often set the tone for the marriage. It is a man responsibility to pay the bill on all dates, PERIOD!

3. Abstain from any attempts to have sex prior to marriage. If you want to have sex, it's time to get married.

Any man who is dating a woman to have sex with her does not care about her or himself. **Every human being knows in his spirit (conscience) that pre-martial sex is wrong.** Pre-marital sex has disastrous consequences on your spirit, mind, emotions, and physical body. Sex is a spiritual activity, which joins together spirits and makes a man and woman one flesh. **Sex makes marriages legal. This process is and should be reserved for those who have totally committed themselves to**

each other under the covenant of marriage. If you are ready to have sex then you should get married and do it the RIGHT WAY! It is selfish to take a woman's body without committing to her all that you have in marriage.

A man must keep himself out of positions in which he is vulnerable to his attraction or the advances of a woman. There is not enough willpower in the world to save a man from his desire for a woman. Therefore, it is important to stay out of those positions, which will put pressure on you to have sex with a woman you are not married to. A real man cares about a woman he is dating and respects her body. It is wise for a man to save himself for his wife.

4. Dating is not an audition for a shack up partner.

<u>**No man should ever move in with a woman!**</u> This shows poor judgment and a lack of self-esteem. A man was not created to live off a woman's resources. Cohabitating is a cheap replication of marriage. Research has shown the devastating consequences of cohabitation:

- Cohabiters experienced significantly more difficulty in their marriages with adultery, alcohol, drugs, and independence than couples who had not cohabited. Apparently this makes marriage preceded by cohabitation more prone to problems often associated with other deviant lifestyles – for example, use of drugs and alcohol, more permissive sexual relationships, than marriages not preceded by cohabitation. (Michael D. Newcomb and P.M. Bentler, "Assessment of

Personality and Demographic Aspects of Cohabitation and Marital Success," *Journal of Personality Assessment* 44 (1980): 11-24).

- The National Sex Survey reports that cohabiting men are nearly four times more likely than husbands to cheat on their partner in the past year and while women are generally more faithful than men, cohabiting women are eight times more likely than wives to cheat. (Judith Treas and Deirdre Giesen, "Sexual Fidelity Among Married and Cohabiting Americans," *Journal of Marriage and the Family* 62 (2000): 48-60.)

- The National Marriage Project reports that while the poverty rate for children living in married households is about 6 percent, it is 31 percent for children in cohabiting homes, much closer to the 45 percent for children living in single parent families. (David Popenoe and Barbara Dafoe Whitehead, "Should We Live Together? What Young Adults Need to Know about Cohabitation Before Marriage," *The National Marriage Project*, Rutgers University, 2002, p. 9.)

Cohabitation is not a part of dating.

5. Be honest.

Always tell the truth. Lies hurt people's feelings, not the truth. To avoid unnecessary emotional problems, always tell the truth to the one you're dating.

6. Do not date anyone you are not interested in marrying.

You should never date a woman you know you have no interest in marrying. Now you ask, how do I find out whether I like her or not with out dating her? The answer is following the "**Safe Dating System.**"

- First, observe a woman from a distance. It is important to not let her know you are watching her because she will likely make adjustments and show you only what she wants you to see.

- If you decide to purse her after observing for an extended period, if possible (certain situations require you to act quickly), then approach her as a gentleman. Begin telephone conversations or an e-mail relationship, preferably both. Spend time communicating to explore her **personality, family background, life goals, interest, values, finances, credit history, faith or religious values, marriage and family views**.

I believe it is extremely important to find out as much surface information as possible before ever attempting to date. This is a responsible and very safe way to find out if you would like to pursue a dating relationship with her.

I encourage you to **stop wasting time**! <u>As a man, you want to spend your time and invest money into dating the woman you know that you're going to marry</u>. (This is a high return investment!)

7. Date only one woman at a time.

Men should never date more than one woman at a time. This is irresponsible and shows unwillingness to commit. Living like this does not build strong character. Think about it, if you cannot be married to more than one woman at time, then you should not date more than one woman at a time.

8. A man must have his own transportation.

<u>Under no circumstances should a man ever rely on woman's transportation for a date.</u> Remember, the purpose of dating is to court (prepare for marriage). A man should not take advantage of a foolish woman who chooses to spend her gas and time chauffeuring him around or allowing him drive her car. This is out of order. If a man does not have his own transportation, then he should not be dating.

9. A man should not drink or do drugs on a date.

No man should use drugs or alcohol of any kind on a date. The primary purpose of drugs and alcohol is to change a person's mental perception. With drugs and alcohol in a person's body, you cannot see the true character of an individual. Most men drink toxic substances on a date to enhance their personality or to have a "good time."

    Some men use alcohol or date rape drugs to take advantage of women. It shows bad judgment and a lack of concern for the woman by being intoxicated on a date.

Drinking alters your mind and can cloud your judgment in situations that may call for you to protect her. Drinking jeopardizes her safety. **Do not put your date's life at risk by drinking or doing drugs on a date.**

10. Do not take a date to a bar.

Taking a woman on a date to a bar is not wise. Any woman who wants to go on a date to a bar is likely not the woman you want to marry. The bar is full of people who want to feel differently about themselves and their lives. There is not one happy person at the bar, **not one**! However, many people choose to manage their emotional hurts and disappointments with alcohol and cigarettes.

There is not one person alive who does not know the harm of alcohol and cigarettes, yet they go to the bar and drink liver damaging chemicals while blowing harmful tobacco chemicals in each other's faces.

The effects of cigarette smoking are still destructive and very widespread. (U.S. Department of Health and Human Services. The Health Consequences of Smoking: A Report of the Surgeon General. U.S. Department of Health and Human Services, Centers for Disease Control and Prevention, National Center for Chronic Disease Prevention and Health Promotion, Office on Smoking and Health, 2004.)

Remember, dating is intended to prepare both parties for marriage, and a bar is not a good social activity that helps to prepare for a successful marriage.

11. Do not talk on your cell phone while on your date.

This indicates that your date is not your primary priority. Talking on the phone while you are out with your date is flat out rude and neglectful. Your date should be important enough to focus all your attention or she is not the right one.

12. Do not ever take advice on your relationship issues with ungodly, unmarried or miserable people.

Misery loves company. You want to take advice or counsel only from people that have the manifestation of what you want in your life. Do not take advice based on people's opinion or their experiences. It is wise and safe to receive counsel according to the Word of God.

13. Be a gentleman.

A man should always be a gentleman. A man should always open the door for a woman. A man should help the woman with her coat, pull out her chair, and allow her to be seated first. Allow your date to order her food first. Men should not walk in front the woman as if he is leaving her. A man should always open the car door for her and assist her in and out of the vehicle. When you walk on the street together, a man should always walk on the outside of the street protecting her from oncoming traffic. This should be a way of life. Following these fundamental principles will help you develop in character and become a better man.

Lesson 11
What Every Man Must Do Before You Get Married

It has often been said that the first year of marriage is the hardest. However, the Bible offers us some wise advice on what a married couple should do for the most successful results in the first year of marriage. The book of Deuteronomy (24:5) advises that a man should be free of all his responsibilities in life and stay at home with his wife for **ONE year** to bring happiness and cheer, and to get to know her. From this marriage principle, two things are very clear.

1. It is obviously implying that a man would have his business together before he takes a wife. The only way a man will not need to work for money is if he already has wealth. Typically, a married man's family provides him with the blessing of a home and cash.

2. Secondly, it clear to us that it was never intended for a man wife's to work a job. If the man is not at work in the first year, why would a woman be?

These are the principles that we believe give newlyweds their best chance to experience success from the beginning of the marriage. **This is why the first year of marriage has been so difficult for so many people**. As I stated before, when I got married, I was working four jobs trying to make sure that we had enough. We did not have a lot of time for each other as newlyweds — this was marital suicide. This places a great responsibility on the husband to gain financial education to find out how to make money work for you, instead of having to spend 40 percent of your day away from your wife, simply because you do not have enough money. The more time you can spend together, the better your chances are for marital success. The wisest advice I can give a man who is not married as of yet is to prepare financially. The first year is critical to the foundation of your marriage, and it is vital for men to take the time up front and get to know their wives and focus on pleasing her FIRST. These are 15 precious principles that I would suggest that every man understand before getting married.

1. Know what your purpose is.

Purpose is what develops and guides a family to levels of great fulfillment and happiness. Again, we encourage every man to find and live out his purpose. We suggest finding your purpose before you get married.

2. If you are not ready to serve your wife, then do not get married.

3. Understand that the ring is important.

The engagement ring is very important to the woman because it is a symbol of being chosen. An engagement ring says, "Someone loved me enough to ask my hand in marriage, and I said yes." This is why a man must find out what kind of ring his future wife wants and find a way to get it for her. Foolish people try to convince couples that the ring is not important, but **THAT IS A LIE.** All women care about the size and beauty of the ring because it says a lot about how her husband views her. No woman should ever sell herself out and say, "A ring is not important!" She's saying that only because she believes that asking for the ring she really wants will scare off her potential husband. This is a major cause of marital failure because it sets the bar for the marriage. It is not in the size of the ring, but in the value of the ring to the person who is receiving it.

4. Get your finances in order.

A man should have his financial situation stable enough so that his new wife is not forced to work to contribute finances to "your" family. It is the man's responsibility to provide a quality life for his future wife. No man should marry a woman and expect her finances to contribute to his household economics. A true husband understands and enjoys the responsibility of caring for his wife. This attitude will take you to the next level of marriage.

5. All Couples Need Counseling Prior To Marriage.

Many men have ignorantly believed that counseling is only for people who have problems; however, God told us that we all need counsel to establish our purpose in life (Proverbs 15:22). Every couple needs a wise counselor (preferably a husband-and-wife team) to counsel them prior to marriage. Many men have foolishly avoided counseling because they do not want correction, and these marriages always fail very quickly. Do not be foolish and think that you do not need counseling. Every couple needs wise counsel from a married male counselor or couple that have the results that you want in your marriage. A wise counselor is going to ask you hard questions and get all in your business. That is what you need to succeed. It is very destructive to go into a marriage with secrets and being secretive. Before marriage, every issue must be discussed in full and truth detail and a wise counselor can help you do that.

6. Prepare a solid living arrangement.

Preferably a house, but your first married living arrangement must be one that the husband provides. **DO NOT MOVE INTO A WOMAN'S HOUSE.** A woman does not respect a man who moves into her house.

7. Nuptials (Formal Ceremony) with a priest and witnesses.

Contrary to popular belief, the wedding ceremony is for the public. Weddings build faith and encourage others to follow suit. When people selfishly leave the country or go to the justice of the peace, they rob family and friends of the blessing of sharing what should be the most special day of your life.

The purpose of the priest or minister is to counsel you throughout your marriage and to hold you accountable to God for your marriage vows. The priest's job is to bless the union with his words, his faith, and his spiritual endowment that come only from a man of God. A wedding chapel minister or justice of the peace are authorities only in legal terms. They have no authority to pronounce **the blessing** over your marriage as your pastor that knows you can. Many people get married at the justice of the peace, in Las Vegas, on a tropical island, away from most family, friends and their lifelong local church to avoid correction. Typically people go to these places to avoid being questioned or hearing the truth. In most cases, it is the woman who arranges the marriage (which can never work) in this situation or a man trying to be cheap. However, whatever the case is, these marriages are never fulfilled because they lack the spiritual blessing that comes from the order of God. **I'm not suggesting that a marriage performed by a justice of the peace or away from the local church and priest cannot survive**; I'm clearly saying that the marriage will always lack, unless this error is corrected. If this is you, I'm warning you that your marriage must be submitted to God, not a court-appointed employee. There is no blessing operating in a marriage that was performed in selfishness. **Weddings are very important.**

8. The wedding plan.

Regardless of what you have been told, a wedding is not about you, it is about your future. Women plan their wedding from the time they are little girls. Most women know how they want it to look and every single detail of the wedding. Allow your future wife to have the wedding of her dreams. If you are asked to contribute or pay for it, do it with an attitude of understanding. Do not go into debt for a wedding, but go over and above to make sure your future spouse is very pleased. If you cannot fully provide a proper marriage ceremony for your bride, then you should not be getting married. A marriage ceremony is very vital to a marriage union. Again, Las Vegas, justice of the peace, or Caribbean island weddings generally are a sign of desperation, impatience, cheapness, selfishness, and fear (of others opinions). Contrary to foolish opinion, we should make our wedding day as special as it can be. The marriage process is the foundation for your marriage, and the wedding is as big of a part of it as getting counseling and financial planning. Understand that you are sowing seeds into your future. What do you want to grow? You should plant only what you want to grow. You should be thinking and believing that you will be married only once. The wedding celebrates the value of your future wife. Every man should desire to give his wife a huge celebration.

9. Plan the honeymoon.

Ask your future wife where she wants to go and make it happen. Search for the absolute best deal through Priceline.com, Netscape, gotrump.com, and other online travel groups.

10. A husband must never place family members or friends before his wife. Especially his mother!

Many men have foolishly placed their mother ahead of their wife and caused strife and contention in the marriage. The first principle of marital prosperity is that a man must leave his mother and father and firmly cleave to his wife (Genesis 2:24). If a man fails to do this, then his marriage is always open for failure because his wife does not respect him. Every man must never place anyone above or before his wife. These issues must be settled prior to marriage or we can guarantee that your marriage will fail miserably.

11. Obtain full insurance before you get married (life and short-term disability).

Fully insure your family with a life insurance policy, short-term disability, auto and home (or renter), health and dental insurance. Protect your family against any unforeseen accident or occurrences.

12. Honestly assess your relationship with God.

God should be first in your life, and then he can be first in your marriage. To be successful in life and marriage, a man needs God's guidance and wisdom.

13. Identify a more mature married couple to model and receive correction from.

14. Truthfully and fully discuss child planning.

Openly talk about the number of children you both would like to have. If possible, agree to a number, but always be open to more or less. Also, discuss methods of birth control before having sex on your honeymoon. ** **Husbands, I suggest that you do not put your wife on birth control pills. Birth control pills disrupt her normal bodily functions, and husbands should consider the harm these pills can do to your wife.**

15. Spend as much time together as possible.

I want to encourage couples to act on these principles and seek counsel from more mature married couples who have followed the path of marital victory. I failed in my freshmen year of marriage and continue to fail because very few of these things were in place before I got married. Not until I was properly taught by my mentor did I turn my situation around. You have a leg up on me now. Use this information and prosper.

Lesson 12
The Roles & Responsibilities Of A Husband

Despite of what society is trying to tell us, in marriage, there are defined marriage roles and responsibilities. I firmly believe that if you know what is expected of you, it is much easier to meet that expectation. This law will provide men with a clear list of 20 roles and responsibilities that come along with the office of the husband. Because so many men have not been raised in the home with their father, a great deal of men go into marriage relationships lacking knowledge of what roles and responsibilities a husband is expected to perform in the marriage relationship. These basic principles will help men clearly understand their God-given roles and responsibilities.

The Roles & Responsibilities Of A Husband

1. A husband must love and value his wife.

2. A husband must know his purpose (the will of God for your life) and God-given vision (plan).

If a man does not know what God expects of his life or what God wants him to do, he will destroy his family.

3. A husband must never argue back and forth with his wife.

Husbands, take your rightful place as the example for your wife by being the peace keeper in your home.

4. It is a husband's job to spiritually develop his family.

- The husband is the pastor of his home.
- Pastors feed the sheep.
- A husband is accountable to God for his family.
- A husband must have the right motives.
- A husband is not a dictator.
- A husband operates with integrity.

5. A husband must guide the direction of his household by speaking words of life and peace over his wife and children.

A foolish man curses and disrespects his wife and children.

6. A husband must abundantly provide for his wife and children.

It is not a woman's role or responsibility to work to provide for the home. Your wife got married for you to take care of her, not for you to use her money. A wife's role is to be a compliment to her husband and build upon the foundation he already has in place. Very few wives want to work for other people, but they are afraid to admit it. Wives are supposed to help their husband in his service to humanity. However, wives have taken on a larger role in the workplace because husbands have failed to do their jobs. Many wives are forced into the workplace for money to meet the family's needs and her own personal wants. The world system, society, bad advice, poor parental examples, and personal experience have led married couples away from the original plan for marriage.

Certain men have oppressed and misused their wives, but a wife should be more independent with her husband, not a captive. A part of a husband's role is to set his wife free from the cares and responsibilities of this world. Every woman has gifts and talents that their husband is responsible to develop. Women often bury themselves in a job or a career and never reach the purpose and potential inside of them. A wife's first responsibility is to her husband. Therefore, her husband is required and should enjoy providing his wife with an abundant supply of resources to enjoy life, and not stress out paying bills. Women should not be working harder than their husbands. It is a part of the husband responsibility to happily provide for his wife and children.

7. A husband must work and not be lazy.
Laziness always brings poverty. A woman has no respect for a man who does not work hard and take care of his family. A lazy man does not deserve a wife, or any sex from her.

8. A husband's job is to intercede, supplicate, and pray daily for his family, leadership, and others.

9. A husband must always seek wise advice.

The stupidest thing a man could ever do is take advice from anyone who does not have the results of what you want in your marriage. Do not ever take advice or discuss your marriage issues with ungodly, unmarried, or miserable people. Only take advice or listen to people that have the manifestation of what you want in your life.

10. A husband must bring closure to all unresolved emotional issues and leave his past behind.

A man who brings his past family issues into his marriage will create a huge mess and the marriage will fail.

11. A husband must never speak or entertain divorce as a solution to marital issues.

A husband must decide that divorce is not an option.

12. A husband must be committed to pleasing his wife.

Every husband should desire to make his wife happy all the time. The same passion that you possessed as a boyfriend must be continually renewed daily.

13. A husband must be more mature than his wife.

14. A husband must save money and build wealth.

It is your responsibility to have short-term disability and life insurance to ensure that your wife and children are adequately provided for in the case of tragedy.

15. A husband must have patience with his wife and children.

16. A husband must submit to his wife.

- **Submit means** to yield yourself to the authority or will of your wife.
- Submission is an attitude of the heart. (There is no murmuring or complaining.)
- Submission is not unquestioned obedience to your wife.
- <u>**Submission is willingness to follow leadership as long as it doesn't violate your values**</u>.
- **A wife will have a difficult time obeying and submitting to her husband if he is not following his purpose.**

17. A husband must protect (mentally, emotionally, and physically) his family.

This requires a man to have a strong prayer life and operate in the wisdom of God.

18. A husband must adultery-proof his marriage by using good judgment with excellent moral conduct while interacting with other woman.

19. A husband's job is to develop his married sex life by building a love making environment.

20. A husband must be an example for his children.

- A husband must raise his children with honor and integrity.
- A husband must make choices that will bless his children's lives.
- A husband must always be loving and caring toward his children and not provoke or discourage them.

These are the primary roles and responsibilities of a husband, and I've found that when men do these things, the marriage works out much better.

Lesson 13
The Roles & Responsibilities of A Father

Again, God has given fathers 10 primary responsibilities in their children's lives:

1. To protect his children.
This creates emotional stability and a sense of safety.

2. To discipline his children.

3. To provide financial means for food, clothing, college, entertainment, toys, weddings and extracurricular activities while he is living, and to leave a bountiful inheritance when he dies so his children's lives are not financially difficult.

4. To build and maintain his children's self-esteem.
A father has the role and responsibility to impart value, self-worth, courage, boldness, a sense of purpose, and confidence into his children.

5. To provide guidance. To provide financial, emotional, life, and social education.
Fathers should be the primary counselors and advisors in their children's lives.

6. To teach children the proper respect for their mother.

7. To keep the virginity and sexual purity of his children.
All sexual dysfunctions (adultery, fornication, molestation, homosexuality or rape) are directly connected to our emotional relationship with our father.

8. To be directly involved in the marriage process of his children, giving away his daughter and preparing his son for being a husband.
Fathers' failure in this area is the reason so many marriages are failing today.

9. To be a role model and example for his children in his conduct and choices in life.
All children imitate their fathers.

10. To provide his children with unconditional love.

All of these attributes are what a father means to his children. If a man fails in these roles and responsibilities, his children and those they marry will suffer all of their lives. If your father did not do these things for you, it does not mean that you cannot succeed in your career, ministry or life goals; however, it does mean that you will have a spiritual and emotional void that can be filled only by God. Children follow the examples of their fathers, good or bad, and if you as the father do not follow purpose, neither will your children. Using drugs, smoking cigarettes, having **multiple** babies out of wedlock by different partners, whoring, shacking up or being an adulterer, drunkard, liar or thief sets a horrible example. You should not be surprised if your children do the same things.

Fathering ultimately comes down to fathers being living examples to their children. Children do not do what their fathers say, but what they see their fathers do. Following the wrong example of our fathers passes a curse from generation to generation. Whether your children start their lives blessed or cursed is up to the choices you as the father makes and how you live in front of them.

All people have to identify the truth about their relationships with their fathers. Internally, every person knows whether he got what was needed from his father. Failing to be honest about this relationship will leave you seeking the fulfillment and validation that can come only from your birth father. People carry this baggage all their lives, and it makes them emotionally unstable. This is one of the most misunderstood issues in life. People never figure out what is driving their decisions and their need to validate themselves. Because their fathers failed to provide them with love, guidance, protection, honor, financial security, and self-esteem, they had to seek it on their own. People use sex, alcohol, food (for many this is the source of being overweight), drugs, church, work or school to cover up the pain of being rejected by their father. Every individual alive has to bring emotional closure to his relationship with his father, particularly if the relationship or lack thereof was a hindrance to him as he developed into an adult. This pain must be addressed, or you cannot move forward in your life.

If I Don't Have A Father In My Life, What Do I Do?

Men must understand that the most influential relationship in your emotional, spiritual, and mental development is with your father. The real reason men act so lost and have no sense of direction is because their **fathers have failed** them. Our fathers are supposed to be our source of love, affection, confidence, security, finances, dependence, and spiritual guidance. Our father's most important role is to teach us how to live according to the Word of God. If he fails or does not live what he is teaching then women and men alike are left to seek other means of understanding and spiritual guidance. This is why so many men rely on opinions, bad advice, television, movies, and their education to be the source of their decision-making process because they have no foundation in life.

If this is you, I encourage you to **settle** (bring closure, address the truth, or forgive him) your relationship with your father. Now is the time to deal with all of your past emotional, mental, physical, and sexual abuse. If your father has sexually abused you, had you out of wedlock, cheated on or beat your mother, it is time to address it. **Whatever the circumstance is, the time has come to speak the truth in love, forgive, and** move forward. You will never have peace until you settle your issues with your father.

Write down how your father influenced your life, whether positive or negative.

_____
_____
_____
_____
_____
_____
_____
_____
_____
_____
_____
_____
_____
_____
_____
_____
_____
_____
_____
_____

Lesson 14
Every Man Must Stay Under The Authority Of A Senior (Mature, Wiser, And More Established) Male

In addition, regardless of your age, every man needs to be held accountable by a more mature and wiser male. The problem for many men is that they were not raised by their father. Every man requires protection, instruction, and guidance from a father figure. If any man is unwilling to receive correction, instruction, or reproof from another man, then I can guarantee you that his life and marriage will be a frustrating failure. All men must consistently be corrected, counseled and advised to fulfill their purpose in life. All men must willingly submit to a more mature male authority figure to have a success life and marriage.

Write down a list of men who have had a positive influence on your life.

_____
_____
_____
_____
_____
_____
_____
_____
_____
_____

Lesson 15
Grow Up!

Gentleman, it is time to grow up. No real man should ever look, talk, or act like a boy. Too often grown men are still living out their boyhood dreams at the expenses of their wife and children. Immaturity is dangerous and will place you in a situation that is not profitable. Personally, I want to challenge every man to expand beyond sports and the hip hop image of themselves. While it may be profitable for Allen Iverson or Jay Z to have braids or wear a du rag, a husband and father of three with two jobs may want to reconsider it. Men have to go beyond depending on their mothers to do everything for them and grow up and be a man. A real man is self-sufficient, requiring no aid or support to get his job done. Most men do grow and develop to the point that they need a wife, but wise men learn how to live on their own, solve problems, and succeed individually before taking a wife. In my view, this is the number one problem among today's generation of men. Men have to take life seriously and be aggressive about being a success, and stop make excuses. I hate excuses and refuse to associate with any man who likes to make them. A man who makes excuses is unteachable. Now is the time for men to step up, be men and teach our sons how to be men. This is the only hope we have of changing the state of our nation and local communities.

Men have to understand that it is not a woman's job to raise your children, protect or

provide for her family, it is ours. As men, we have to get our priorities straight as individuals before we can be successful as husbands and fathers. I am challenging every husband and father to step up and accept the challenge of taking better care of your wife and raising your children with honor and integrity. Gentlemen, you must understand that your life and priorities have to change when you become a husband and father. **Your friends or family members are not more important than your wife and children.** Men, it is time to grow up! I encourage you to challenge yourself to develop strong character, self-discipline, and an unbreakable will to succeed in every area of life.

This book is the beginning of the male education and empowerment movement that must occur if we expect to save our next generation. Being a man is the hardest job in this lifetime, but with manhood education, men have a greater chance of success. I hope this book encouraged you to be the *Best Man* you can be.

Dr. Jesse W. Jackson III

M.A.N. School®
7 Laws
Of Male Success

Dr. Jesse W. Jackson III

Introduction

America is facing the greatest social crisis in its history – fatherless homes. Sadly, millions of boys are growing up in homes without fathers to teach and guide them. Many more are being raised by men who were not taught how to be successful. Men must be taught how to be men by a man, based on sound male success principles. These principles cannot be taught by women. They must be taught by men who model them. When boys are not taught how to be men by a man, they often are underdeveloped and lack character. Another problem is that many fathers who are present in the lives of their children were not taught these principles. Therefore, they cannot teach these principles to their sons, and this has created a dangerous cycle of failure.

Society needs men to MAN UP and accept the challenge of being leaders in the home and workplace. Men must be taught to step up financially and take care of their family, thus taking the burden off women. As fathers, we have failed this generation of young boys. This is why this generation is so angry, bitter, violent and emotionally unstable. This is the reason these boys use crime, gangs, sex and marijuana as their medication to hide their pain. If we continue at this rate, our women will be left completely unprotected, and our children will not reach their full potential in life.

The world's number 1 problem is lack of strong male leadership. To address this massive problem that men all over the world are experiencing, we must attack and change the ideology of how we view and train men. Men are not brute beasts who lack self-control and must have sex with every woman who will let them. All men have the potential to be wise sons, excellent husbands, responsible fathers and strong leaders. After-school programs, prison, the military and medication are not solutions for this epidemic of malehood illiteracy; but male education, accountability, male guidance, mentoring and empowerment are the answer.

The Solution

Every man has to answer these questions. What kind of man are you? What are your goals in life? What is your plan to obtain these goals? Based on a man's character make up he will either be a m.a.n. who:

- makes excuses
- always blames someone else
- never accepts responsibility for his life or actions

Or he is a M.A.N. that:

- Makes No Excuses
- Always accepts responsibility for his life and actions
- Never quits or gives up

These basic principles will decide how successful you are in life as a man. Fathers have God-given responsibilities to educate, protect, guide and set a good example of success for their children. Men have to be taught how to do this. Men need a basic philosophy of how to succeed in the life as a man.

There is a new way to educate and empower males for success in life and that is M.A.N. School. Man School is based on Seven Foundational Laws of Male Success accompanied by various lessons on how to work these laws. My research of this topic has shown me that there are 7 fundamental laws or principles for male success which are:

- Find Your Purpose And Live It.
- Watch Your Mouth And Keep Your Word
- Maintain Sexual Self-Control And Practice Other Good Health Habits.
- Be A Leader, Not A Follower.
- Become Financially Free.
- Find A Wife, Love Her And Give Her The Best Life.
- Raise Your Children With Love And Affection, And Leave Them An Inheritance.

These are the 7 Laws of Male Success. These valuable laws will provide men and boys of all ages with proper guidance that will produce success in education, health, business, finances, marriage and fatherhood. I learned all of these laws after becoming a major failure in my life. I had plenty of men offer me their personal experiences and theories on manhood, but very little of it produced success. There is more to manhood than having sex, watching sports, making money, and having children. Men have to be taught how to be "good" men, husbands and fathers. God's intent was for our fathers to be our teachers. If you are a man who is without a father or who has lacked an appropriate male role model, this book will be a tremendous help to you. **If you are a mentor or a coach to another man, understanding and teaching these laws are critical.** These laws will offer guidance to any man or boy who is willing to learn and will produce purpose, educational, health, business, financial, marital and fatherhood success.

Our goal is to inspire ten million men to action by taking the "Best Man Challenge," which is to live and teach the 7 Laws of Male Success. **Inspiring change in ten million men will impact one billion lives worldwide.** I feel a divine call to duty to inspire my fellow brothers to stand up, evaluate their lives, and make changes and step up to a higher level. Our women and children need us. A boy without a father is like a solider without a gun at war; his chances for success are limited. **The Best Man challenge is for this moment in time. This nation is going through tough times, and in tough times, leaders (men) have to rise to the occasion.**

I wrote this book to empower men of all ages and stages in life, <u>but this book was especially designed as a leadership manual for men who want to be great</u>. These are the undeniable principles of manhood who will make boys into men, help good men become great, and help men who have missed it find the mark. **I give you the Best Man charge:**

get this book in the hands of every man you know and discuss it. Send books to prisons, juvenile detention centers, group homes, head start agencies and schools all over the world. The Best Man Revolution has begun, and I need your help to save the United States and families all over the world by inspiring 10 million men to action. Thank you for taking the Best Man Challenge. Let's get started!

Law 1
Find Your Purpose And Live It

The first law of male success is to ***Find Your Purpose And Live It.*** This country needs men to know and understand their God-given purpose for living. Men must understand that our primary responsibilities for living are to protect, guide, and develop our wives and children. This is a principle that must be taught everyday to men of all ages. Men need purpose and focus. Without it, our families will continue to suffer and society is completely doomed.

Mankind was created by God, in the image of God, and his divine purpose for every man was for man to:

- Have control over his environment (not people); this is why we fight over territory, laws that govern the territory, and how we should live in the territory.
- Work by thinking, planning and speaking — this is why our words are so powerful.
- Be married, have a God-given wife, and use sexual intercourse for pleasure and to reproduce himself by having children. When a man takes a wife, he must depart his from his parents and reprioritize all of his relationships because his wife now comes first.
- Influence everyone around him.

- Operate his body on fruits, vegetables, and grains (every herb bearing seed).
- Be a steward of wealth.
- Protect his family in the environment.
- Guide his family.
- Develop his family.
- Have discipline and follow his God-given purpose.

When men are taught these basic truths, they can govern their lives accordingly. When men do not know or live by these truths, it can be very destructive and nonproductive.

It is important to know that every person alive has a God-given purpose. Before we are ever born, God sets our destiny. God has a purpose for our lives, yet most men have disregarded God's purpose and adopted their own. You will NEVER be fulfilled until you find and carry out God's purpose for your life. As men, we must do what we were intended to do or we defeat our purpose for living.

I found my purpose after I was inspired to attend a church service at the Word of Faith International Christian Center's Convention. It was June 20, 2003, and Bishop Keith A. Butler was teaching on finding your purpose. I felt like he was talking to me for the two-hour sermon. I believe I heard an inter-voice that prompted me to review my life. I began to see that, to become the man I wanted to be, I needed to disassociate myself with certain people, quit several of my jobs and stop coaching sports. I immediately broke down crying because I knew it was time for me to be a man and let go of my childish games.

I had grown comfortable in my role as a basketball coach. Anybody who knew me back then will tell you that coaching basketball at Detroit Noble Junior High School was my first love. I did it with much passion for more than six years.

Although coaching fulfilled my personal dreams, I got further away from what I was born to do. I coached youth sports for the wrong reasons. I used coaching to falsely validate my self-worth and avoid the hurtful realities of my family circumstances. I knew it was time to step up and take my life seriously. After that day, I made the decision to cut off everything and everybody who would prevent me from fulfilling my purpose. I became a student of good ideas and spent more time in prayer daily. Prayer was especially vital for me to find my purpose. As I found my purpose, I began to see how to get order into my life.

My purpose is first to be an excellent God-honoring husband and father. My purpose is to love my wife and bless her all the time. My purpose is support my wife in all of her dreams and the vision that God has given her, and to raise my children in the nurture and admonition of God so He can have more soldiers in the earth. My purpose, secondarily, is to teach, guide, motivate and inspire men in finding and carrying out their purpose for their lives. Finally, my purpose is to finance and publish empowerment education and literature through every available media option so it can go forward all over the world without resistance.

Finding my purpose has provided me with priceless direction that I never had in my life. Today in my life, I do only those things that fall in line with the purpose God sent me to this earth for, and not what I think is a good idea.

I encourage you to take the time to find out why God created you, what his purpose is for you. Following purpose leads to a blessed life, which makes us rich and adds no sorrow to us.

Every man has a divine purpose for their life, and without fulfilling it, they can never be truly happy. I suggest that every man take the time to find his purpose through quiet time (prayer), meditation, and soul searching. A good life is waiting on you, but it starts with your decision to live a purpose-directed life.

Take some time and think about what your life's purpose is. When you're done, write your purpose statement.

_____
_____
_____
_____
_____
_____
_____
_____

What Are Your Goals?

Goals should be based on purpose. Purpose develops mission. Mission develops desire and desire will produce goals. List some of the goals you have in these specific areas. Also, include your plan to accomplish these goals.

1. Life goals

_____
_____
_____
_____

2. Family goals

_____
_____
_____
_____

3. Health goals

_____
_____
_____
_____

4. Financial goals

_____
_____
_____
_____

5. Educational goals

_____
_____
_____
_____

6. Service to humanity goals

_____
_____
_____
_____

Law 2
Watch Your Mouth And Keep Your Word

The second law of male success is to commit to keeping your word. All men must be taught to be a man of his word. As men, all we have is our word. We must do what we say we are going to do. Our word is our bond. Not keeping your word is not a small thing. If our word does not mean anything, then we are worthless and cannot be trusted.

On the other hand, we must also watch the words we let come out of our mouths. Words are very powerful. A word out of your mouth may seem of no account, but it can accomplish nearly anything — or destroy it! By our words, we can ruin the world, turn harmony to chaos, and throw mud on a reputation. Words set things in motion. Most of all, the wrong words can make us a failure in life. Men have ignorantly chosen to believe that words mean very little in our lives, but this is absolutely untrue. Words can move mountains or build roadblocks. If we believe the words we speak in our hearts, we are going to have what we say. Our words shape our lives. Your life today is a reflection of the words you have been saying in the past. Here are some basis truths about the power of our mouths and the words that come from it:

- The tongue of the wise is health.
- A good word will make a heart glad.
- Pleasant words are as a honeycomb, sweet to the mind and healing to the body.

- A fool's lips cause contention, and his mouth calls for a beating.
- A fool's mouth is his destruction, and his lips are the snare of his soul.
- A man's [moral] self shall be filled with the fruit of his mouth; and with the consequence of his words he must be satisfied [whether good or evil].
- Death and life are in the power of the tongue.

If you want a different result in life, it starts with our words. To be successful, you must only speak what you want to happen in your life and situations. If we believe the words in our hearts and put action to our words, things must change. Never forget that a man's word must be his bond.

Law 3
Maintain Sexual Self-Control
"Keep It In Your Pants"

The third law of male success is *Maintain Sexual Self-Control And Practice Other Good Health Habits.* Millions of men have been taught that being a man means that they can and should have sex with as many women as possible. This mentality has destroyed millions of men and their families. How many men have been ruined and families destroyed because of a lack of sexual self-control? How much money has been lost through lawsuits, child support, legal fees, and court costs because of a lack of sexual discretion? If someone ever took the time to add up these numbers, it would be staggering.

    Rape allegations, paternity suits and adultery scandals have ruined the reputations of some of America's brightest leaders and icons including former Detroit Mayor Kwame Kilpatrick, NBA Legend Michael Jordan, Tiger Woods, Tupac Shakur, former New York Governor Eliot Spitzer, and former U.S. President Bill Clinton. Millions more have experienced extreme financial hardship because of child support, have gone through divorces because of adultery or have contracted an STD because of a lack of male sex education. It is time to dispel the myths of manhood that teach men to have sex with as many women as possible and set men on a path of sexual understanding and responsibility. Ignorance is very costly. **If a man cannot control himself and make wise decisions**

about his sexual conduct, his life will always be full of unnecessary problems. This law will teach boys, single men and married men how to make wise decisions that will protect their family, financial resources and reputation against s*exual indiscretion.*

Law 4
Be A Leader, Not A Follower

The fourth law of male success is *Be A Leader, Not A Follower.* Men of all ages must understand that society needs men to be leaders not followers. I believe that men have a responsibility to be leaders, whether it is in his business, politics, education or the military. However, every man has a primary leadership responsibility in their own home first. After years of leadership research and practice, I have found that every male leader must possess these four non-negotiable character traits to be considered for any level of leadership.

1. A true leader must be faithful to his wife. If a man will cheat on his wife, with whom he is in covenant with, then he is a threat to cut anyone's throat. A man who is unfaithful to his wife is not trustworthy and should never be trusted to lead anything of value.

2. A true leader cannot be a thief. How can we trust a thief? If a man is proven to be a thief, then he should be disqualified from all leadership positions.

3. A true leader cannot abuse alcohol or other mind alternating substances. If a man chooses to drink alcohol and use drugs, he puts himself in a vulnerable position to poor discretion in situations with loose women. A drunk always has an excuse for his behavior, and real leaders do not make excuses. A leader who likes to drink alcohol is a risk to sell out those he is leading when he gets drunk.

4. A true leader must rule his house well. If a leader does not have the respect of his wife and children, he is not qualified to lead. If a man's children do not respect him, he has clearly failed at home and needs to spend more time there before can guide someone else.

These leadership principles should be observed by all leaders, including government officials (presidents, Senators, governors, mayors and Congressmen), husbands, pastors, principals, policemen, sheriffs, coaches, CEOs, and all management. I believe if we hold leaders to these standards, our businesses, schools, churches, and governments would dramatically change for the better immediately.

Law 5
Become Financially Free

The fifth law of male success is to take control of your financial future. What is your financial situation? Are you broke? Are you living paycheck to paycheck? Are you about to lose your home to foreclosure? Are you working two or more jobs, but getting nowhere? Do you have a plan to achieve financial freedom? If any of these are you, don't live another year in financial oppression.

Financial responsibility is vital to every man's success in life. Without the understanding of financial education and intelligence, a man will always be broke and keep his family broke. The American financial system is a complete failure. It is designed so that someone will always be left behind. Don't let that be you and your family.

Many have asked me, "Why is being a financially free part of the Best Man Challenge?" The truth is that having money is a requirement of being a man. A man without money can offer very little to his family and society. Men need money to help their families. It is the lack of money that causes men to send their wives to work for money, not to develop potential. It is the lack of money that causes young men and women to go into debt just to get a college education to better themselves. Money's purpose cannot be debated. This challenge is for men who want to go beyond the bare necessities of life. This is for men who want to live blessed and be a blessing to others in need. Becoming a financially free will put you in a position to offer your family the best life and empower less fortunate families with educational and employment opportunities. For a true Best Man, being financially free is required.

Become An Honest Employer And Create Great Jobs

One of the areas where I believe we need the most leadership is the market and workplace. **We need men to be leaders who create jobs, instead of look for them.** We need men to become honest employers to create great-paying jobs. Over the past three decades, the work place has deteriorated because the marketplace no longer operates on the character ethic; it operates on the "do whatever you have to do to get ahead" ethic. Our places of employment lack integrity.

Many of today's employers cannot be trusted. The workplace has become about "self," and no one is looking out for the working class. While I am a true capitalist, I believe in the working class. I know that, as a capitalist, we must take better care of our workforce. We need better jobs, with 100 percent benefits packages and fair wages. Employers must spend time investing in the personal development of their workforce. Great employers want to see their employees succeed in their personal lives. They encourage employees to find and develop their gifts and talents and start new businesses.

Today's workplace is oppressive. Many employers don't care about their employees. They lie, cheat, steal pensions, create stressful work environments, hire abusive supervisors and make unexpected layoffs. Most companies are top heavy, with administration receiving big salaries, while the workers barely make it. The challenge is to be an employer that empowers its workers to be better people. It was once said that 99 percent of all employees want to do a good job, but the leadership is unable to support them, thus it never happens. This why the Best Man Challenge wants to educate and empower men with the tools they need to be successful business owners.

Become A Life-Long Learner

Learners are earners! Men must become more proactive in educating ourselves. We must spend more time reading and improving our writing skills. So many men don't invest in personal education; this means health, finances and relationship development. As men, we spend too much time watching sports or going to watch women take off their clothes. However, we are not investing enough time into becoming smarter, i.e. expanding our vocabulary, learning about money and improving our health. Most men go to work, come home, eat, watch TV and go to sleep. The Best Man Challenge is designed to inspire men to read books and listen to audios that will make us better husbands and fathers, while also making us healthier, smarter and richer. Learners are earners!

Law 6
Find A Wife, Marry Her, Love Her And Give Her The Best Life

The sixth law of male success is ***Find A Wife, Marry Her, Love Her And Give Her The Best Life.*** Men must find one wife, love her, and give her the best life. For so many men, this has been extremely difficult because they have not been taught these principles. Most of us were taught to "get as much as you can." This philosophy has destroyed families and cost men their fortunes in divorce, child support and alimony. Marriage was designed to be between one man and one woman. There is one perfect woman in this world for all of us. Our job is to find her, and when we find her, to love her, then we must marry her and give her the best life.

    Now, this obviously requires education and training. When I got married, no one told me how much goes into being a husband, and that is why I failed. Being a husband requires consistent training like our bodies do. So many men get complacent when they get married, and the opposite should be happening. They should get more motivated to love and care for their wife. This book will share the basic roles and responsibilities of a husband; however, in the third book of this series, *Happy Wife Is A Happy Life*, I will talk extensively about how to love and care for our wives at a consistently high level. This challenge is focused on educating and empowering men to love and care for our wives and give them the best life possible.

Law 7
Raise Your Children With Love And Affection, And Leave Them An Inheritance

The seventh law of male success is ***Raise Your Children With Love And Affection, And Leave Them An Inheritance.*** This challenge is focused on bringing fathers and their children back together. I know personally that many men truly love their children, but don't know how to love them because their father was not in their life. America's No. 1 problem is fathers being absent emotionally and physically from the home. All children need unconditional love from their fathers. This builds self-esteem and confidence to be successful in life, and this is what so many of us lack.

Also, fathers have a job to leave an inheritance for their children and grandchildren. This is another reason men must have money! How much easier would our lives be if our fathers had given us a financial stipend to start our life with and pay for college? These types of things make the difference in a child's life.

Finally, as men we must realize that we are the foundation of this earth and must take our place as the wise and mature "head" of the household by living lives that will bring honor to our family. You can do it! The purpose of this book was to guide boys and men in the principles of manhood success. Boys and men of all ages are experiencing the greatest challenges in the history of mankind. All men need guidance, support, encouragement and, most importantly, love from another man, particularly their father. I believe this book is an act of love and will provide men with the essentials that they need to have success in every area of life. I hope this book has inspired you to make wise decisions, analyze your life and make changes where they are necessary. These are the laws that every father must teach their sons. If your father is not in your life, I suggest that you use this book to guide you in how to be a successful man and raise sons. This book is the beginning of the male education and empowerment movement that must occur if we expect to save our next generation. Being a man is the hardest job in this lifetime, but with manhood education, men have a greater chance of success. I hope this book encouraged you to be the *Best Man* you can be.

Dr. Jesse W. Jackson III

The Best Man Daily Affirmation

I am a man. I make no excuses. I take full responsibility for my life and my actions. I never blame others for my problems. I protect, guide and develop my environment. I will find (or have found) and live my purpose. I am a life-long learner. I have and practice sexual self-control and discipline. I practice good health habits. I am financially wise and very responsible. I build wealth for my children through honest and passion-felt business endeavors. I will find (or have found) one wife, love her and give her the best life possible. I will raise my children with love, affection and leave them a healthy financial inheritance. I am an example to all men through my conduct. This is my contribution to society.

About The Author

Jesse W. Jackson III is one of America's foremost professional counselors and educators in the areas of 21st century professional development, leadership and teamwork. Dr. Jackson is an internationally recognized professional development expert, consultant, speaker, and international best-selling author. His organization has trained thousands of professional staff and leaders worldwide. Dr. Jackson founded and built Best Man, LLC into one of America's top performing professional development consulting firms. Dr. Jackson has authored twelve books, several of which have become international bestsellers, including the male development classics; *The Best Man, College or Prison: The Male Crisis of The 21st Century, 21st Century Leadership & Teamwork and Success Or Failure: Teachers Are The Difference*.

Dr. Jackson received his bachelor's degree (B.A.1997) in Psychology, and his master's degree (M.A.2002) in Counseling from Wayne State University. In 2008, Dr. Jackson received his Ph.D. in Counseling from Trinity Institute.

Dr. Jesse W. Jackson III has counseled and consulted for more than 50 companies and addressed more than 20,000 people in 100 talks and seminars throughout the United States. As a keynote speaker, seminar leader and licensed professional counselor, he addresses more than 100,000 people each year. He has excelled in helping school districts and organizations find effective solutions to keep male students in the classroom and improve academic and social achievement.

Over the past year, Dr. Jackson has been providing guidance for collegiate and professional athletes throughout the country in the areas of marriage, domestic violence, alcohol and drug abuse, sexual misconduct, and violent criminal conduct. Dr. Jackson is currently consulting and providing professional development training for government and human service agencies throughout the United States. Dr. Jackson focuses on improving the workplace environment, customer service, the productivity and leadership skills of the 21st century employee and workplace leader.

To invite Dr. Jackson to speak at your school, business, organization, church or special event, contact him:
Jesse Jackson III
P.O. Box 210973 | Auburn Hills, MI 48321
Website: www.jessejackson3rd.com
Email: info@jessejackson3rd.com
Phone: 1-888-841-4267 Fax: 888-215-6481